Chapter 1: Advocates for the Underdog

Since this brilliant world we live in is comprised of astonishing people, many individuals pass up possibilities in light of cultural inclinations and stereotypes.

In certain circumstances, this additionally involves lifting up the people who are less advantaged because of area and social class. This section will analyze inventive individuals who have committed their lives to tracking down these astonishing individuals and propelling their station.

Vikram Vora, CEO and CoFounder of MyDentist

Vikram filled in as a sales rep of dental hardware in the last part of the 2000's. As he headed out from one facility to another, he saw how displeased the clients were with the stand by times, valuing, and poor gear. Vikram started to think about what might work on this clearly fruitless, however important, business model.

In 2010, he sent off MyDentist. Vikram put together his new dental centers with respect to a bistro model. Patients were given low fixed costs on methods, foreordained holding up times, and cutting-edge hardware. Obviously, this was generally welcomed by the common who couldn't be served by the past model. The primary variable of which was cost and time constraints.

In barely three years, Vikram's thought has extended to 72 facilities serving the average the whole way across Mumbai, India. By setting up his centers around the passenger train stations in Mumbai, Vikram has met individuals right where they are. The centers are additionally compatible in that any strategy can be finished at any of them. For instance, assuming a dental embed is started at an area near a patients' home, however advantageous for them to finish at a facility near their work, this is without a doubt conceivable and a consistent process.

Vikram has achieved something not happening elsewhere on the planet. His organization utilizes 280 full-time dental specialists and dental collaborators, as well as 120 advisors who all come from average families and have been prepared by the company.

Princess Reema Bint Bandar Al-Saud, CEO of Alfa Intl.

A princess and an inventive mastermind, Princess Reema comprehended that main portion of individuals in Saudi Arabia were utilized in the labor force. The a large portion of that were jobless comprised totally of ladies. Saudi Arabia is known to be one of the most un-moderate countries on the planet, and welcoming ladies into the labor force was unbelievable. Conservatives see this as a revolutionary act.

Over the most recent two years, Princess Reema has enabled ladies in her organization, Alfa Intl., which is an extravagance retailer in Saudi Arabia. She has ventured to such an extreme as to supplant experienced sales reps with ladies. New regulations were passed by the Saudi government to manage the regions where men had the option to work in the retail area. For instance, men were restricted from working in undergarments and corrective shops that main served female clients. This made new regions for female employment.

Princess Reema is the little girl of Prince Bandar, a long-lasting minister for Saudi Arabia in the United States. Accordingly, she experienced childhood in Washington
D.C. Yet she keeps now that she is down home that she isn't trying to Westernize her nation, however develop it into more present day ideals.

Even however Princess Reema was intending to invest some energy as a homemaker, the Harvey Nichols store run by her organization in her old neighborhood of Riyadh was in desperate need of renovation.

This brought about a total destroying of the area and making facilities for her labor force of ladies. The organization gave transportation since most Saudi ladies are taboo to drive vehicles. They likewise took into account childcare on location to assist laborers with engaging the "who will watch the kids" argument.

Accordingly, Princess Reema has not been liberated from reaction in her city of Riyadh. The Harvey Nichols store area, likewise the first to open outside of the United Kingdom, has encountered a 42% drop in income. This is expected in

part to the high volume of ladies utilized as well as a blacklist by those faithful to the previously mentioned experienced sales reps. Still Princess Reema is sure that the social insight will change.

From Princess Reema we can learn that social change must happen and can be initiated by the empowerment of people who are wrongly perceived to be inferior.

Catherine Hoke, Founder and CEO of Defy Ventures

How would we be able to bring potentially the most peered down on individuals of American culture and lift up them to significance and independence? It is an overwhelming endeavor, yet Catherine Hoke has demonstrated that it's conceivable. As indicated by a review directed in 2005, almost 68% of state detainees who were delivered were rearrested in three years or less. That number soar to almost 77% inside five years.

The brutal truth is that individuals who are set free from jail have next to no open doors when they get out. As an undeniable criminal, positions are challenging to stop by, and those that are reachable are generally the lowest pay permitted by law positions. Previous cheats and street pharmacists struggle with this reality and frequently return to a daily existence a crime.

Catherine had a revelation in the wake of visiting Texas detainment facilities in 2004. She saw how lawbreakers coordinated themselves inside their wrongdoing circles similar as a company is set up. She chose to concoct a method for putting those abilities to legitimately utilize. The abilities were at that point there, they were simply being utilized for some unacceptable reasons.

Catherine began a business program in the Texas jail framework. After moving to New York, she established Defy Ventures and fostered a six-month program that shows previous prisoners the essentials of beginning their own organization. The members are associated with field-tested strategy rivalries and are launch into a three-month hatchery period to see their thoughts come to fruition.

Since it began, Defy Ventures has delivered 115 alumni. 71 of those graduates have proceeded to make their own organizations. So what's next for Defy Ventures? Catherine intends to take the program public and help

previous prisoners all over the United States.

Catherine teaches us that finding the right solution for people that society has been unable to help is a win- win for America. Not only does she employ the unemployable, she indirectly creates additional jobs in the economy.

(Sources: http://www.nij.gov/points/redresses/recidivism/Pages/welcome.aspx)

Jose Maria Alvarez-Pallete, Founder of Wayra; Coo, Telefonica S.A.

In 2010, Jose went through the Silicon Valley in California. He was astonished at the number of Latin-American software engineers and fashioners he met on his outing. This left him with an inquiry. For what reason did they need to migrate to America to find lasting success in the tech business? This left his organization, Telefonica, requesting supplies and programming from abroad.

An innovative individual like Jose just requires being given a need prior to thinking of an incredible arrangement. He knew that for his organization to develop, the encompassing tech economy would need to develop also. In 2011, Jose sent off his thought called Wayra, a South American local word significance wind. In something like a half year, Wayra was ready to go. Before the finish of its first year, it had foundations set up in seven nations across the globe.

Wayra got a lift in 2013 as much as $13.4 million from Jose's other organization, Telefonica. It currently flaunts 14 foundations and has arrived at an achievement as one of the world's biggest gas pedals of new companies in under two years.

Jose saw that he could build an ecosystem for his

own endeavors while accelerating others in an area that required people to leave their country to succeed.

Chapter 2: Advancing the Internet and Mobile Web

Computers have turned into a basic piece of our lives as have cell phones. We are continually carefully associated with a web that gives us admittance to practically the whole world at any given moment.

This is the aftereffect of the absolute most inventive scholars ever. All things considered, the Internet and Mobile Web have made a stage on which a whole age of creatives will make their fortunes. This is the thing we can gain from them for those of you who are all the more actually inclined.

Michael Heyward, Founder and CEO of Whisper

We are right now going through a period when protection and obscurity are sacrosanct contemplations. Into a web-based existence where it appears to be each road needs to share your information comes any semblance of Whisper. Murmur is a portable application where clients can admit their privileged insights under the cloak of namelessness. Like plunking down in the confession booth with a great many clerics who don't have the foggiest idea who you are.

Michael Heyward created Whisper to keep computerized trails arriving at impasses. Clients type out confidential and overlay it on a significant picture. The substance is then added to a data set served to a large number of different clients ordinary. Murmur doesn't have client profiles or a stage to follow different clients. Correspondence is had through private unknown messages or by posting one's own mystery in light of another. The serious deal here is having the option to remain totally unknown assuming that is what you want.

So what application flaunts 3.5 billion site visits a month outperforming the New York Times site for an entire quarter? Truth be told, Whisper.

Michael Heyward shows us that we can battle unwanted intrusions on any level with a simple rebuttal...even with a whisper.

Sean Rad and Justin Mateen, CoFounders of Tinder

Sometimes advancement isn't tied in with making another idea, however rather

working on a current idea.

Online dating is enormous, yet Sean and Justin needed to figure out how to make it less confounded. Conventional web based dating locales include finishing up a broad profile and addressing a huge load of inquiries to be coordinated with potential love interests. While this model has worked for millions, it isn't the best thing in the world everybody. The profiles are frequently so broad, they don't pass on a lot to be examined during the "get to know you" period of dating. Additionally, the people who aren't leaned toward nitty gritty correspondence are left pondering a great deal of things.

Tinder is a portable application that brought the dating site profile down to a solitary picture and diminished introductory correspondence to a straightforward swipe of the thumb: Right for yea and left for nay. Justin says this point of interaction "catches the second when your eyes interface with somebody." It brings that part of meeting somebody eye to eye into a computerized setting.

Users of the application are ensured of shared fascination since Tinder possibly tells them assuming the two players swipe right. There has been extraordinary accomplishment with this straightforwardness with 10 million matches and 750 million swipes by clients consistently. Sean and Justin have intends to create the application further with more tomfoolery and cheerful highlights in the close future.

Tim Kendall, Head of Product at Pinterest

You don't need to be Internet and Social Media sharp to realize that Pinterest is tremendous. What you may not know is assuming your business is intended for ladies and you are thinking about Pinterest, it would be a very sharp move. Why? Since 80% of Pinterest clients are ladies and they produce 92% of the things stuck. Pinterest additionally has exhibited its impact to business sectors both on the web and off.

Cha-ching!

So where does Tim Kendall become possibly the most important factor on all of this? As the Head of Product at Pinterest, Tim was instrumental in sending off the Pinterest application for the iPhone, Android and tablets in 2013. It wasn't simply the arrival of the applications however, it was the way that applications permitted pins to show more data to versatile clients. This soared Pinterest traffic and 75% of that traffic currently comes from a versatile device.

Tim took something that worked, made it better, and

then made it compact subsequently increasing the value of a generally tremendous company.

(Source for Pinterest details: http://marketingland.com/report-92-percent-pinterest-pins-made-ladies 83394)

Alan Schaaf, Founder of Imgur

Content is ruler of the Internet. Before, that content alluded essentially to composed content. Once the power of images were realized on a number of levels such as marketing, engagement and entertainment, they became a staple as well. It's insufficient just to have the option to utilize pictures on the web, yet sharing pictures is additionally generally popular.

Even with Social Media overwhelming the web, old mediums are as yet famous like message sheets, discussions, and social bookmarking locales like Reddit.com. The greater part of these stages don't permit space for picture transferring. Enter a picture have like Imgur.

Alan has taken incredible measures to guarantee that Imgur is the main picture have on the net. It's loaded with highlights and permits remarking and private informing between clients. Moreover, clients who simply need to loosen up can involve the site without signing in and view pictures simply by tapping the Next button.

Imgur flaunts 130 million novel hits each month as a money box of viral pictures and images. It's essentially an interpersonal organization for picture sharing. Alan's development has made Imgur one of the most well known locales on the Internet.

Alan instructs us that you can involve a similar thought as another person and make it something incredible by improving it. He's focused on the development of Imgur and molded the site to fit how its crowd utilizes it.

Chapter 3: **Innovations in Creative**

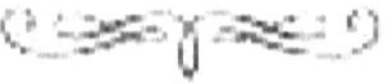

Renewal

Whether actually recharging for you is upcycling, making something old new once more, or something totally unique, there is no question that reestablishment of any sort takes advancement and imagination. The tales in this section will presumably make you feel good inside and maybe motivate you in a little inventive restoration of your own.

Roger Norris Gordon, CoFounder and President of Food Cowboy

Forty-three billion pounds of food decay in trash dumps every year since it gets wounded or harmed en route to neighborhood merchants. Assuming you consider widespread starvation rates, this is ridiculous. Roger wasn't willing to allow it to work out. Obviously the conveyance of this food to those in need is too costly an undertaking for the organizations transporting the produce.

What did Roger do? He hopped on his PC and assisted his sibling and numerous other transporters with observing a permanent place to stay for their undesirable burdens at covers near the drivers' areas. Then he started thinking about Mobile technology and how most, if not all, trucks have smart phones. This could make the simplicity of finding an area for their harmed, yet at the same time palatable take as basic as sending a message message.

In 2012, Food Cowboy waS conceived. Roger and his sibling established the organization which is basically a web application that permits drivers to be matched to neighborhood covers where they can drop undesirable food. The food gets into destitute hands and is kept out of the landfill. Many drivers have joined. Together they have saved in excess of 500,000 pounds of food. This has collected consideration from the U.S. Division of Agriculture who trusts an exhibition regarding the matter will bring more thoughts like Roger's.

Roger recognized a need and filled it with a waste. In so doing, though, he stopped a shameful waste of life- giving food.

Michael Phillips Moskowitz, Chief Curator at eBay

In 1995, eBay was established in a San Jose front room. From that point forward, it has been an Internet staple. You would likely be unable to observe an enthusiastic Internet client who doesn't have a sign in for this goliath online yard deal. Since its commencement, it has developed and advanced throughout the long term, yet figured out how to keep up with the model with which it began.

Secondhand customers are not generally restricted to neighborhood shops. They can shop the world for treasures among someone else's undesirable items.

So, what could be better? Michael figured out how to feature the coolest things he and his group viewed as with the help of curation. Content curation is only an extravagant term for getting sorted out happy in a rundown or under a particular topic and introducing it in a significant manner. Anybody with an eBay sign in can get to Michael and his group's assortments like "Retro Redux" or "The Natural World".

Michael's assortments are something other than records. Michael centers around the story and retells that story as a piece of each assortment he assembles. The story sells the things and brings a large number of clients searching for his rundowns. He makes a significant encounter to go with every thing he organizes and that sells merchandise.

Michael's recognition that the story is just as important as the items connects with an audience who feels the same way. This personal connection makes Michael's creative renewal innovation a success!

(Sources:
http://www.cs.brandeis.edu/~magnus/ief248a/eBay/history.html
http://www.bethkanter.org/content-curation-101/)

Billy Parish, CoFounder and President of Mosaic

When it comes to petroleum derivatives and clean energy, there is a ton of discussion. As individuals, we perceived quite a while in the past that we expected to relinquish petroleum products and continue on toward cleaner, sustainable power sources. This progress presently can't seem to occur; notwithstanding, with advocates like Billy Parish, we will start to witness such changes more quickly.

Billy is completely mindful that the explanation our change to clean energy is so sluggish is

in light of the fact that petroleum derivatives create an amazing measure of income for fuel organizations. At the point when he sent off Mosaic in 2013, that's what he affirmed "The shift from petroleum derivatives to clean energy addresses one of the biggest abundance creation chances within recent memory, in the event that we can democratize responsibility for assets."

That's actually the thing Billy looked to do with Mosaic. It's really a group subsidizing stage that interfaces financial backers with sunlight based projects that are under-funded. Anybody who has just $25 to spend, can contribute. This has delivered $7 million for business projects, however Billy hasn't halted there. In mid 2014, Mosaic started financing advances for homes too.

Billy broke down our hesitation, found a solution, and moved forward to innovate in the much-needed area of renewable energy. The Earth will thank him one day.

Theaster Gates, Artist, Founder of Rebuild Project, and the Director of Arts and Public Life at the University of Chicago

What do you get when you blend craftsmanship in with a preference for good culture? The response is Theaster Gates. Theaster began at a private level on the South Side of Chicago when he really wanted a spot to live in 2006. He has changed void homes into social spaces. He additionally transformed a previous lodging project into homes and a center for the arts.

Theaster's most recent undertaking is the change of an old bank incorporating into a library that will house a chronicle of African-

American history. Likewise, it will likewise incorporate a café. This will accommodate a critical need on the South and West sides for a spot to get a beverage and a decent meal.

Simultaneously, Theaster is likewise handling a goliath craftsmanship project for the Chicago Transit Authority. As opposed to get into a particular subject for the undertaking, Theaster has banded together with region radio broadcasts to make content to rouse inhabitants to consider new ideas about what sort of workmanship this venture ought to incorporate. Theaster presumes that thusly, he will cultivate imaginative authority rather imaginative production.

Theaster has sought to include culture in the public space in a big way because he knows that culture

should be central to how the human landscape functions.

Chapter 4: **Taking Entertainment Forward in a New Age**

With the beginning of such countless roads to make, diversion isn't just about TV, radio, and music any longer. A huge development has occurred somewhat recently that has introduced the Internet and mobile phones as large players in the diversion game. A marriage with customary media has made this content streamable to Smart Tv's, cell phones, PCs, and tablets. Everything is a hybrid nowadays and we'll discuss developments in amusement in this chapter.

King Bach, Comedian

The cool thing about the Internet and diversion are each of the stages that spring up from thoughts and take off. Like structure a piano and observing somebody who improvises, these stages simply resound for certain individuals. They have a skill for engaging crude ability. It's continuously surprising to observe those individuals who have taken an instrument or stage and dominated it.

Andrew Bachelor has in excess of 9 million supporters on the well known video stage, Vine. Is astonishing that he's acquired that continuing in a little more than a year under his client name King Bach. He's involved the six-second time breaking point to set up a good foundation for himself as a comedic force. A month after his Vine debut, he had a million followers and a deal with United Talent Agency.

Andrew isn't halting there. He's pre owned Vine to sling his profession into TV. He's a standard on Showtime's House of Lies. He is likewise chipping away at an impending task with Adult Swim and has grabbed the eye of a few different joke artists. His huge accomplishment on Vine drove him on to TV and made him a central part in the advancement of entertainment.

Andrew tried something new, found he had a knack for it, and rode his raw talent into huge success that is just beginning for this young man.

Jenji Kohan, Creator of Orange Is The New Black

Netflix. Need we say more? The mail DVD rental organization turned web based video administration has endorsers during the many millions. The numbers keep long-laid out link premium channels like HBO honest. In 2011, Netflix set it sights on making unique substance, and by 2013, had hit the jackpot with House of Cards. It couldn't beat that, or could it?

Enter Jenji Kohan and her creation Orange Is The New Black. The show debuted in the Summer of 2013 without an excessive number of assumptions. Jenji was simply having a good time since she was at that point the maker of Showtime's Weeds, a modestly effective endeavor of a show about marijuana.

So how would Jenji be able to manage a New York setting, a cast of new ability, and some experimental writing? The outcome was an enormous amazement hit in Orange Is The New Black. It's a merging of dramatization and parody in the setting of a womens' jail. Jenji searched out under-used ability for the female-dominent jobs. She then set about composing a show that she saw as engaging, and in this manner has pleased millions.

Netflix is famous for not delivering numbers like viewership, but rather Gigaom.com detailed that in excess of 60 million individuals have pilfered episodes of the series utilizing distributed networks. Obviously, Jenji's magnum opus was restored briefly and third season up until this point. She's prepared herself for the strain and says she's simply attempting to "make the best show possible".

Jenji took a concept, fleshed it out with lesser known actors, and turned it into an overnight sensation proving great things come to those who give talent a chance.

Sources: http://en.wikipedia.org/wiki/Netflix
https://gigaom.com/2014/08/20/orange the latest trend dark downpour insights/

Tim and Karrie League, CoFounder of Alamo Drafthouse

Let's not fail to remember the Silver Screen. From our past review including Netflix, clearly film rentals are as yet a practical industry. Nonetheless, it's not simply having the option to watch at home. Theaters are likewise still suitable individuals from the film business in general. They've been no different for quite a long time; go to the theater, purchase a ticket, perhaps get some popcorn, and watch the most recent films

from Hollywood.

So, how should one approach expanding the film insight? Why, incorporate grown-up drinks and a feast obviously! That is actually the thing Tim and Karrie have finished with their Alamo Drafthouse. It wasn't to the point of simply making the setting however, they additionally have a film appropriation organization called Drafthouse Films. You may be leaned to imagine that these undertakings wouldn't prevail without the style of Hollywood or every one of the most recent movies. You would be wrong.

Tim and Karrie have taken the Alamo from one Side of the country to the other and opened eight additional venues In 2013 carry their absolute to seventeen. They desire to have fifty performance centers working by 2017. They're not just branching out though. In 2013, Drafthouse Films' The Act of Killing was designated for an Oscar. They additionally have a yearly film celebration which is one of the biggest in the U.S. called Fantastic Fest. They facilitated the presentation of Forever Fest in Austin which underlines programming made by people for women.

Tim is referred to for his irregular exposure strategies also. He advanced Drafthouse Films by testing the chief, maker, and star to have somewhat of a brew drink-off to see who wet themselves first. Tim lost. He has additionally been generally plugged for his restriction on Madonna because of her feature failure when she was called out for messaging during a screening of 12 Years A Slave. It appears Tim is somewhat of a backer for legitimate moving-going etiquette.

Tim and Karrie took a tried and true entertainment venue and made it phenomenal. Their gamble paid off big time and proves they are in a "League" of their own.

Mario Queiroz, VP of Product Management, Google

For many years, TVs have required some assistance ordinarily as a set-top box or something to that affect. In the last part of the 2000's, the period of the recieving wire at last bowed to this model. Whether you're a link and satellite endorser, or buy into nothing specifically, chances are that you have some sort of superfluous box connected to your TV. Purchasers mixed when SmartTV's hit the market.

A SmartTV incorporated the capacity to get to real time features like Netflix,
Hulu, Amazon, and even YouTube without requiring yet one more box.

One man brought the $200 billion SmartTV industry to its knees when he presented a little arrangement at just $35 a pop. Mario Queiroz took all the additional usefulness of a SmartTV and packed it in the Google Chromecast, a little dongle that squeezes into the HDMI port on most current TVs. At such a reasonable value, the Chromecast was a more useful arrangement than purchasing a new television.

Mario halted the SmartTV unrest with a straightforward gadget that has sold millions. In the mean time, we are for the most part hanging tight for the following huge thing in TV. Nonetheless, meanwhile, we can partake in a plenty of real time features as well as having the option to "cast" streaming web content from any semblance of YouTube, Pandora, and numerous other famous services.

Mario and his team at Google took just eighteen months to take the Chromecast from a concept to market. He came up with a better solution to the problem than a whole new television and he packaged it small with a price tag that packed incredible value. Amazing!

Chapter 5: New Discoveries in Science and Medicine

If humanity were to quit propelling in Science and Medicine, could we go on? It's not likely. Innovativeness isn't just held for the Arts and Entertainment. Each domain of our way of life and being requires innovative reasoning. This book wouldn't be finished without a part to feature a few vital players who are advancing in the vital areas of Science and Medicine.

Jorge Odon, Inventor of the Odon Device

Sometimes arrangements come from the most impossible of spots. Would you be able to envision a man with no clinical preparation fostering a gadget to ease labor in non-industrial nations? That is actually the thing Jorge did. His creation started with an issue as most do. Of the passings that happen to moms in labor, close to 100% of them are because of absence of preparing for specialists and absence of legitimate hardware all in creating countries.

The following period of Jorge's revelation was the consequence of a fairly arbitrary issue. In 2006, Jorge was filling in as a technician and watched his associates show how to eliminate a plug from a container utilizing a plastic pack, which they learned out of every other place on earth, from a YouTube video. Soon thereafter, Jorge woke with the thought: wouldn't this idea work assuming the jug were an uterus and the stopper was a child to aid childbirth?

Jorge went to work and made a glass uterus loaded up with one of his girl's dolls. He took the plan to a Buenes Aires showing emergency clinic where it was gladly welcomed. Individuals at the medical clinic assisted him with applying for the licenses he would require and by Jorge's birthday on March 1, 2011, thirty live preliminaries were sent off by he and his group. They were all fruitful. In 2014, Jorge found employment elsewhere as a specialist to additionally foster the Odon gadget full-time as examination proceeds worldwide.

Jorge took a random idea and developed it into a device to solve a completely unrelated problem. That is

most certainly the consequence of a few inventive reasoning and shows that occasionally, individuals foster astonishing items outside of their picked field.

Chase Adam, CoFounder and CEO of Watsi

There's generally more work to do in the creating scene. Medication is perhaps the biggest field needing more individuals and more development. The way that individuals in these nations get below average consideration or even bite the dust for absence of assets, information, or gear is crazy in the advanced world. Pursue Adam is among individuals making that a more uncommon occurrence.

Chase is centered around finding the high-benefit, generally safe regions where imagination can occur with the clinical field. Any other way it very well may be a delicate subject with protection issues and different elements becoming an integral factor. Pursue accepts that putting more accentuation of the client experience in the medical services industry will take the business a wide margin. While there has been a ton of spotlight on the business to business of the business, little advancement has occurred in the patient realm.

So the thing is Chase doing as his part to make these thoughts a reality? He created Watsi which is a stage for swarm financing. It permits clients to give straightforwardly to individuals looking for clinical treatment in non-industrial nations. Pursue has taken a little piece of the riddle and set up it to take care of the issue of cash for individuals who in any case could go without legitimate treatment.

Chase started with a small area and created a solution to one huge problem. There's no doubt he's working on the next one as this is being written.

Carl Hart, Neuroscientist at Columbia University

Drug misuse and enslavement has been a not kidding issue for quite a while, however is fixation truly as solid as we suspect? Carl Hart has to strongly disagree. He led and distributed a review in 2012 that showed meth addicts would quite often pick $20 over a hit of meth. Carl has likewise done explore that really inclines toward chronic drug use being the consequence of climate as opposed to brain

drive as normally thought.

Carl feels that the term, compulsion, is utilized on too wide a scale and has gone on record against government agents. He's stepped up to the plate against errors in science and approaches that frequently put the oppressed in a difficult situation. Carl draws from his life as a youngster in an unpleasant Miami area in holding that researchers will more often than not describe drug addicts and medication takers as a distinct difference to what he saw developing up.

Carl isn't willing to let trends in science dictate the science behind experience. His research and stance on drug abuse research deserves applause.

Kathryn Hunt, Paleo-Oncologist

What assuming you wound up newly gotten back from an undertaking in Egypt when you figured out that you were experiencing ovarian malignant growth? That happened to Kathryn Hunt. Presently going away, she started assembling the pieces soon after that undertaking. A considerable lot of the bones she was examining had proof of infection. Then there was the ancient record which mentioned cancer repeatedly. There was no substantial proof since there was an absence of clearness on what disease in antiquated remains would look like.

Kathryn and a couple of her partners established the Paleo-Oncology

Research Organization and have since recognized in excess of 230 instances of likely malignant growth in old social orders. Accordingly, they have assembled an open-source data set for specialists to talk about and share information.

Later on, Kathryn is planning to secure financing to concentrate on a portion of those cases all the more profoundly with radiological investigation, as well as, DNA testing. She desires to have the option to recognize designs in the antiquated record and give scientists regions on which to concentrate more intently.

Kathryn fit together the puzzle pieces because of her own misfortune and made leap forwards in the investigation of old social orders and Medicine.

Chapter 6: The Top 25 Lessons You Can Learn From the Most Creative People in the World

1. Problems are settled most frequently by distinguishing a need locally, and satisfying that need.

2. Empowering the apparently substandard individuals in a culture will advance cultural changes.

3. Employing individuals that society considers unemployable makes positive patterns in the economy and in a roundabout way sets out unexpected work open doors for others.

4. When zeroing in on business development, extend your encompassing business environment simultaneously to guarantee longevity.

5. Sometimes retaliating against huge interruptions or assault on an individual or business level need just be refuted with a whisper.

6. You don't need to make a genuinely new thing to improve.

You can enhance by improving on a current idea.

7. Don't be reluctant to develop thoughts that are as of now functioning admirably. You have the capability of making it better.

8. Success doesn't generally come from novel thoughts. At times you can prevail by taking a current thought and making it better.

9. When offering a support to individuals, continually shape your support of the manner in which your crowd utilizes it.

10. Seek ways of satisfying requirements with assets that would somehow or another be wasted.

11. Remember that the story is similarly just about as significant as the sale.

12. Always try to associate with individuals on an individual level.

13. If cash is a hindrance to another development, figure out how to make it profitable.

14. Do not hesitate.

15. Include culture in all that you make. The human scene ought to constantly reflect legacy and functionality.

16. Try everything. On the off chance that you have a skill for something, do it a lot.

17. Be mindful so as not to overlook your own crude ability. Feed it.

18. Utilize ability since it's ability, not on the grounds that there's a name appended to it.

19. Expand on custom. Make it new while saving the old.

20. Solve issues by including more worth and more modest sticker prices. The fortune will be the same.

21. If you overlook irregular thoughts, you could pass up an astounding innovation.

22. Innovation can occur for you outside of your picked field.

23. Start small. Sometimes the smallest ideas solve the largest problems.

24. Do not disregard your own experience regardless of what others say. Depend on it.

25. Adversity can be the best educator. Pay attention to what it's attempting to say and gain from it.

Conclusion

Thank you again for downloading this book!

There you have it. What did you gain from the main twenty most innovative individuals on the planet? What stood apart to you the most? There's truly a scope of individuals from all strolls of life.

Remember how your folks let you know that you could be anything you needed when you were growing up? This is what they were referring to. These individuals are undeniable evidence that you can be anything and that anybody can be an innovator.

Don't stop here! Take those 25 examples and begin tracking down ways of squeezing them into your life. You may very well end up on the following top twenty rundown of inventive scholars with a couple of illustrations of your own to share.

Finally, in the event that you partook in this book, I might want to ask you for some help, could you be sufficiently benevolent to leave a survey for this book on Amazon? It'd be incredibly appreciated!

Click here to leave a survey for this book on

Amazon! Much thanks to you and best of luck!